SINGER'S FIRST AID KIT

PROBLEM SOLVING FOR SERIOUS SI

by Lis Lewis

T0085636

FIRST AID

ISBN 978-0-634-02595-2
(w/ Female Voice CD)

ISBN 978-1-56922-195-2
(w/ Male Voice CD)

CREATIVE CONCEPTS
P U B L I S H I N G

EXCLUSIVELY DISTRIBUTED BY

HAL•LEONARD®
C O R P O R A T I O N

7777 W. BLUEMOUND RD. P.O. BOX 13819 MILWAUKEE, WI 53213

Visit Hal Leonard Online at
www.halleonard.com

for Myles, who is my greatest gift

Thanks

Finally, I have an opportunity to publicly thank some of the people who have helped me through my years of being a musician and a teacher:

• Thanks to my wonderful and musical family, Irving and Frances Kantor and my two sisters Dana Marsh and Marjorie Kantor who have always enthusiastically supported me. And especially to Dana who was my first, and still most important, role model.

• To my lifelong friend Constance McCord, whose keen perspective gets me through many a rough ride, always keeping me honest.

• To Myles Lewis, my wonderful son, so wise for his years, who I've always been able to count on for insight and love.

• To my dear husband and editor, David Frye, who has endless faith in my ability to accomplish the next task.

• To Jason, Stephanie, Davíd, Kristina & Anisa, who have brought me so much joy.

• To Wendie Colter whose vision and determination got *The Singers' Workshop* started and whose friendship keeps me going.

• To Phil Spinelli who, with loving guidance, pushes me to take the next step.

• To Matthew Niblock for getting out the red pen and making me toe the line.

• To Jerry Lewis, who taught me that art is in the details.

• To the bands I've been in and the musicians I've worked with.

• To my great voice teachers, especially Eugene Lawrence in San Francisco and Robert Edwards in Los Angeles.

• And to my wonderful students who have taught me so much.

Thank you.

What's In This Book

The Singer's First Aid Kit is geared toward singers of all styles of pop music and musical theater, whether your goals are to be a major recording artist or just to have fun at your local karaoke bar. Being a singer, or an artist of any kind, comes with built-in challenges:
- rejection, the ultimate dirty word, can paralyze you
- sickness, poor diet, vocal strain, emotional turmoil can all adversely affect your physical instrument
- the struggle with band members, recording equipment, and your own mental obstacles can drain your confidence

The Singer's First Aid Kit is meant to help you past some of the stumbling blocks. It is in two parts: **The Singer's Troubleshooting Guide** and **The Singer's Warm-Up CD.**

The Singer's Troubleshooting Guide is the section of the book which poses some of the kinds of problems you are likely to encounter and some solutions to them. It deals primarily with the physical and emotional challenges of being a singer.

The Singer's Warm-Up CD contains exercises designed to warm up your voice and prepare you for serious singing. It is approximately twenty-five minutes per program. **The Singer's Warm-Up CD** section of the book answers some questions about using the CD, includes a chapter on breath control and a transcription of the exercises on the CD.

Why I Wrote This Book

I have been a singer all of my life. My musical education began with classical piano at a very early age. I finally stopped taking lessons when I was sixteen because I didn't enjoy learning in an atmosphere where my personal tastes and ideas seemed to be unimportant. I taught myself guitar and didn't touch the piano for another ten years. I always felt there was something inherently wrong with a method that didn't take the person's own musical intuitions into account. It took me years to trust my ability to improvise on a melody because I hadn't learned to have faith in my musical instincts.

Later, I was in many bands ranging in style from blues to bluegrass to pop to jazz. In order to have material to sing I became a songwriter. I recorded, performed in clubs and concerts and I toured. It was a great life. After losing my voice on a six week tour (in the third week!) I started taking voice lessons, and after years of training I started teaching.

Being a working singer and teaching at the same time honed my technique: I was always applying what I was teaching by singing in some noisy, smoky club till 2am or by recording in a studio on their 'down-time' between midnight and 7am.

I found that there is so much more to learn as a professional singer than simply the technique of singing: how to put a band together and keep it running, all of the business and legal aspects of the music industry, how to write great songs and much more. While there are many books about songwriting and the music business, there is very little written about the physical and emotional demands of being a singer. Having struggled with them myself, and then having watched so many of my clients in similar situations, I wanted to describe the pitfalls I saw, to help others avoid them.

There is a central self-knowledge that is essential for a healthy career, an understanding of what you, and you alone, can bring to the music. With this comes an acceptance of your limitations: when to say the song is too high or that your voice is too tired to keep singing. These truths give you confidence and the ability to make decisions from wisdom rather than ego. I wish someone had said them to me. Thus, this book was born.

The Singer's Troubleshooting Guide

6 ▷ Vocal Health

Vocal Health

"We kind of got back to the way it should be.
Everything's about being healthy and everyone's working out. . . .
We've spaced out the dates so we have a little time between shows.
It's been amazing…Touring's everything I love.
You eat, you sleep, you play shows.
What more could you want in life?"

Gwen Stefani (No Doubt)
from the LA Times

Photo Credit: Chris Cuffaro

Vocal Health 7

What are the things I shouldn't eat before I sing?

Why doesn't Celine Dion talk for the entire day of her gig?

How can I be heard over the roar of the band?

How much should I practice?

Since your body is your instrument, and you don't get to trade it in for a new model when it wears out, you have to take care of it. As my voice teacher used to say, "treat your voice like an honored guest". House it, feed it, exercise it, give it a comfortable bed and it will work well for you for years.

Sleep, diet and exercise are the essential elements. The image of the rock star who never sleeps, eats only junk food, snorts cocaine and drinks himself to death is the image of a person with a very short career. Sleep is critical if you want to have the tremendous amount of energy it takes to sing, especially if you are singing on a musical theater stage without a mic for eight shows a week, or standing in front of a drummer in a rock band. If you have ever tried to sing on only four hours of sleep, you know how fast you can get vocally tired. And once you start getting tired, you tend to use muscles that are better left alone and that, in turn, makes you even more tired.

Exercise

Regular physical exercise helps increase your air control and power. It also improves your energy, and the muscle tone of your body in general. The better physical shape you are in, the more responsive your body is when you put heavy demands on it, like singing in the recording studio for six hours or rehearsing all day. Also if you are on tour, a regimen that includes exercise helps keep your mind alert. No sleeping till noon and then watching TV till the gig. Get outside and run.

Diet

It should not be too surprising that what you put into your body affects your voice. After all, your instrument is built in and if you are run down or sick, it will not function very well. Apart from helping you look and feel better, eating well gives your body the nutrients and stamina that it needs to provide your voice with strength, endurance and flexibility. There have been volumes written about healthy diets so I won't go into that here. But there are some specific guidelines that singers need to know. A singer's vocal cords need to be wet. Several things cause dryness:
- caffeine or any other stimulant
- alcohol
- smoke (first or second hand)
- a salty diet
- antihistamines or decongestants (they're designed to be drying)
- diuretics
- allergies (if you have food allergies avoid those foods for at least four hours before you sing; if your allergies are airborne, look into herbs and vitamins that strengthen your immune system)
- dairy products (they tend to make your mucous thicker)

Water

Make sure your body has lots of water. Have you ever sung and felt your voice was kind of 'skipping' or that your vocal cords were dry? or felt that you had to keep clearing your throat? or when you are sick you might feel like you have mucus on your cords. These are all symptoms of being too dry. When you are sick, for instance, your whole body dries out (remember the doctor saying "drink plenty of fluids"). Your vocal cords can swell up and get stiff making them much harder to move. It will take more air to sing and your range won't be as big. Carry a water bottle around with you (and drink from it) especially if you live in a big city that has smog and other pollutants.

When you have a sore throat or swollen glands, be careful. It doesn't always mean that your vocal cords are affected but it's hard to tell. A chest cold makes it hard to breathe which is crucial for singing, so it may slow you down, but you can usually sing even if you have a cold. Try not to sing if you have a fever. Remember, your cords must stay very wet and a fever raises your temperature and dries you out.

▶ Vocal Health

Each voice is different. Notice what affects *your* singing and work on eliminating the hazards. You may find that you can have four cups of coffee in the morning and sing like a bird at night, or that if you drink coffee in rehearsal you are hoarse in the morning. It's possible you may like the way your voice sounds when it's dried out. So be it. Pay attention to what you eat and drink, how much you sleep and how much exercise you get and see how it affects your singing.

Vocal Abuse

If you go to a football game and scream, or if you are a waiter at a noisy bar where you have to shout over the music, you are damaging the same instrument you are about to use in rehearsal. You can't abuse it all day and expect it to be ready to use in performance. Don't shout. Celine Dion doesn't speak all day before her gig. Once you start paying attention to how you use your voice, you will become more sensitive to how you use it badly.

The most important thing to remember when you are standing in front of amplified instruments (or even ones that aren't) is not to shout. The impulse to try and be heard over all that sound will overdrive your voice and you will lose it.

There are some solutions. Make sure you have good monitors that are facing you and that are turned up as loud as they will go without feeding back. If the only speakers in the room are facing away from you (for instance, stacked in front of you facing the audience) turn one of them to-

Celine Dion

wards you. Ordinarily, though, there will be two sets of speakers, one for them and one for you. You should be able to sing with a fairly wide dynamic range and still be heard. Don't expect to have all the subtlety you had in the recording studio, though.

But no matter how good your sound equipment is you won't be heard if your band is playing all over your parts. There should be space left in the arrangements for the vocals i.e., the guitarist shouldn't play a lead line while you are singing, the keyboard player shouldn't be playing block chords in the same frequency range as your voice, and the drummer shouldn't ride the crash cymbal all the way through the vocal.

In addition, it is not uncommon for less experienced musicians to play too much and too loud. Instrumental parts should be kept simple and all musicians (you included) need to learn and practice dynamics. If the band roars into the first verse of the song, there is no where to go when the song builds. Unfortunately this is a difficult lesson to learn. It's hard to play quietly onstage with the adrenaline pumping. It's a skill that you will all acquire with experience if you practice it in rehearsals.

Practice & Rest

Get plenty of practice. Sing all the time: in the car, in the shower, while you're washing dishes. When you sing along with a record, turn it down so you can hear yourself. Otherwise you'll never know how you sound because all you'll hear is the other singer's voice.

If you are going to sing in the studio for three hours, you should build your stamina in rehearsal. Start out with a half an hour a day of exercises and then sing some songs and increase slowly to build your endurance. If there is a particularly difficult section of a song, isolate it to work on it. Don't sing the whole song over and over. Most of your vocal practice should be by yourself. Once you get into rehearsals, your vocal technique, the way your body automatically approaches the difficult parts, should be set in your body so you can think about other things.

If your voice is tired, give it a rest. For serious vocal problems, you may need to see a doctor. If you are hoarse, give it a two or three day rest. (Whispering and talking are not resting.) Let it heal. Come back to singing slowly and gently and don't expect to be able to do everything immediately. Practice carefully, noticing the areas of your voice that are damaged. Don't push for sound. Be gentle and work in short spurts - ten minutes singing, ten minutes rest and then ten minutes singing again - until the sound starts coming back without extra air pressure.

Imagine that you had a muscle injury, in your calf for instance. You wouldn't run on it right away. You wouldn't even put all your weight on it for a while. Be patient. This is the only voice you are going to get. Make it strong, powerful and supple by training it and warming up before rehearsals and performances. Get to know it. Treat it with respect.

The Right Teacher

*"There have been lots of different versions of this play
with cast recordings by everyone from Patti LuPone
to Elaine Page to Julie Covington.
All of whom are sopranos and sing in a whole different range than I do.
So I really didn't have that much to guide me musically going in.
On top of that, Andrew Lloyd Webber's score
is very difficult and demanding.
So the first step was to work on singing in upper registers
and to develop a wider range for my voice . . .
It was an experience that I think has had a real impact
on the other aspects of my singing.
In the course of training I wrote 'One More Chance' and
'You'll See,' and if you listen to those songs,
you can hear how I was trying to absorb
and utilize what I was learning."*

Madonna *on training to sing "Evita"
from the Madonna Webpage*

10 ▷ The Right Teacher

Will vocal training make me sound stiff?

Do I need classical training?

Where do I find a good teacher?

How can I get more control without losing my unique sound?

Do great rock singers take voice lessons? You bet they do. It's hard to imagine Tom Petty or Trent Reznor singing 'me-me-me' in a voice teacher's studio. It's easier to think of Sarah McLachlan taking lessons than Melissa Etheridge. Yet, almost every singer you admire has taken lessons at one time or another. It's almost impossible to handle the stresses and demands that a career in singing puts on your voice without learning how to do it right.

As a voice teacher, the questions I hear most from my clients are: if I took lessons would I lose my rock edge? my uniqueness? my raw emotional power? Would I sound like an opera singer? Some singers are afraid that lessons will make them sound too classical, too polished, or not emotional enough. Some are afraid that if they learn too much about it they'll lose their instincts and forget how to sing from the heart.

There are good reasons for these attitudes. Some singers get so involved in the sound of their voices that they forget that their real job is to express how they feel. They get preoccupied with using 'the correct technique'. This generally happens to people who have a hard time being emotional in the first place and are looking for something to concentrate on that will make them feel safe on stage. Their thinking goes, "If my technique was good, then I did a good show."

Tom Petty

Photo Credit: Robert Sebree

Just as it doesn't make sense to get so involved with your technique that nothing else is important, it doesn't make sense to ignore it. A keyboard player who is afraid to learn music theory because it might make him too technical, is limiting what he can achieve. He will reach a point where he is playing the same ideas over and over. Technique and emotion are equally important. Learning to use your voice will only make being emotional easier.

Expand Your Horizons

Singers must learn to operate their instruments like any other musician. Just because it is built into your body doesn't mean you automatically know how to play it. If you could sing freely with power and control you would feel confident and that confidence would give you the courage to try new things, experiment, take chances you wouldn't dare take before.

Lack of information will limit you. You will experience problems without having any idea how they happened or how to fix them. Some of those problems might be: reaching for notes that you don't quite get and straining your voice in the process; singing most of your songs in the same key (which is boring); squeezing your throat to get difficult, high or loud notes which can lead to vocal strain, pitch problems, shortness of breath and

Melissa Etheridge

Photo Credit: Jodi Willie

The Right Teacher

Photo Credit: Joseph Curtice

Trent Reznor (Nine Inch Nails)

lousy tone. You will start to lose notes and get hoarse. In the worst case scenario you could get vocal nodes which require months (yes, months) of complete vocal rest – no talking.

Picture this…you are touring. The agent has lined up the gigs across the country; the promoter has booked the hall; security has been hired; the road crew has set up the lighting and sound and the audience has bought their tickets. The band is ready to play having tuned up their instruments and warmed up their fingers. They are all relying on you and your ability to do your job, but something is wrong with your voice. You just can't sing. You are the reason why the gig must be canceled. It's a nightmare and it's happened more often than you think.

No artist can afford to be in this situation and so almost every artist you can think of has a voice teacher. Of course there are some self destructive artists out there and you've probably heard stories about the tours they've had to cancel or the bands that have fallen apart. One band, having won the opening slot for a major tour, had to turn it down because the singer had blown out his voice. You don't want this to happen to you after working hard to achieve success.

The Right Teacher

Enough horror stories. I assume you are ready now to find a great teacher. On to the next step.

Singing is very personal. You have to trust the person who is going to help you develop your voice. You want a teacher who will encourage you to break new ground, strive toward your goals and develop your instrument as far as it will go. You also want a teacher who will appreciate your uniqueness. You shouldn't end up sounding like a clone of your voice teacher with all the quirkiness and individuality of your voice straightened out. How do you find a teacher who will keep what is unique about your voice but still give you the tools you need to make it better? Let's look at the possibilities.

Teachers can offer a variety of things: technique, coaching, performance work, recording techniques and image consulting. A voice teacher is usually one who works on technique, i.e., the physical skill of using your instrument. A vocal coach might do technique but will also work on song choice, expressive abilities, mic technique and other related elements. A performance coach will help you develop your stage persona; this can include movement, interacting with the band and commanding an audience. An image consultant will guide you in your clothing choice, overall concept and all elements of presentation including assembling your press kit. A teacher who focuses on recording techniques, called a vocal producer, would help you in the studio: how to give an emotional performance while maintaining a great sound, as well as how to use the recording equipment.

You also don't want a strictly classical teacher if you sing rock, blues, pop, jazz, R&B, dance, alternative, country or any other contemporary style. Although the going rumor is that classical training will be good preparation for anything, the fact is that you shouldn't sound like an opera singer singing pop music. Imagine a boxer trying to play basketball and you will get a sense about how differently the muscles have to develop. Good pop voice teachers have taken the basic premises of classical training and adapted them to the rigors of singing in front of a band. Get exactly the training you want right from the start. Musical theater falls between the two categories: either a classical or a pop teacher can work for you if they are familiar with the repertoire.

Ask Questions

Go to clubs and ask for recommendations from the singers you like. (Most of them have voice teachers.) If you are looking for a classical or musical theater teacher, go to the nearest college and ask the music department for recommendations. Look at the ads for voice teachers in the music magazines, then call and talk to them. Ask about their methods, what styles they specialize in, bands they've worked with. Find out their credentials: how long they've been teaching, what kind of training they have, what specialties they have besides teaching vocal technique (i.e., coaching, recording techniques, live performance work.) How long is the lesson, how often do they recommend and what are their rates? Do they record the lesson for you so you will have a tape to practice with during the week?

12 ▷ The Right Teacher

Set up lessons with three or four of the teachers who you liked the best on the phone. This part costs money but it's an investment that is well worth it in the long run. You must find the right teacher because you will be working with them for a long time to come. If you spend a little extra now you can save yourself not only money but the emotional stress that comes from working with the wrong person. On the other hand, if you make a connection with a teacher on the phone and then when you take a lesson with them you feel that they are the right one for you, trust your instincts.

Every teacher has a different style, and for every style of teacher, there are dozens of students who swear by them. But that doesn't mean that teacher is right for you. Some are disciplinarians; some are easygoing. While one teacher may run you through exercises without explaining them to you, another might want you to understand everything that's going on. Some may want to discuss your career aspirations and others only want to work your voice. Some will tell you what songs to sing and others will leave it up to you. There is no right or wrong; whichever style of teacher gets the work done is the right one for you.

Strange New Ideas

When you take your first lesson, be open to your teacher's ideas even though they will be new to you. Singing lessons are about analyzing the physical process of singing in order to improve your voice. To accomplish that, your teacher will have you do exercises that isolate the different elements of your voice. You might not sound as wonderful singing the exercises as you sound singing a song. That's because the exercises uncover the weaknesses that you disguise when you are singing. Remember that a teachers' job is to find those weaknesses and strengthen them. If you only sound good in your lessons, you aren't getting very much done.

If you have questions, ask them. Don't be shy. Try to understand what is going on in your voice and what you should be working on. In the end, it is your instrument and you can't just put it in someone else's hands and say 'do what you want with it.' If your teacher is exercising your upper register and you never sing there, find out why it's important to work on it. If they are having you sing R&B songs when you really want to sing rock, find out why. Maybe they believe you would be a better R&B singer. Or maybe it's all they know how to work on.

Trust your instincts about the teacher. If they talk down to you, if they talk about themselves rather than exploring your needs and interests, or if you just don't like them (personality plays an important part in how successful your lessons will be) find someone else. Once you start, you'll wonder why you waited so long!

Photo Credit: Nick Vaccaro

Suzanne Vega

Practice

"You wake up in the morning and
just be a normal person, ride your bike,
and look forward to playing music, writing songs,
getting into your guitar and getting together with the band."

Eddie Vedder (Pearl Jam)
from Mr. Showbiz,
http://www.mrshowbiz.com

Photo Credit: Anton Corbijn

14 ▷ Practice

How long should I practice?

Should I practice when I'm sick?

Why is it so much easier to sing by myself than to sing with instruments?

Practice every day. If you stop practicing even for a few days you will notice that you start to lose muscle tone just like an athlete. Notes that were easy become more difficult; fast runs of notes get stiff; your tone isn't as stable. Believe the old saying 'if you don't use it, you lose it.'

Practice is done by yourself in a quiet place where you can concentrate on your voice and the right way to operate it. First do the scales and exercises that you have been working on with your voice teacher. Focus on using the muscles that should be working and relaxing the ones that shouldn't be. Go slowly through the weak spots and work on building strength and control. If you do the exercises on automatic pilot you will accomplish nothing, or worse you will reinforce the wrong way to sing. If you are trying to change the way you are singing then you will need to be paying a lot of attention because what comes naturally isn't working.

Next sing a song. Sing it without any accompaniment and try to apply what you've just been working on in the exercises to the song. Break the song down into sections and work a problem phrase over and over. For instance, if there is a high note that is difficult, work on the note by itself. Then work the problem note and the one before it. Often the jump to the high note is the hardest part and if you work it separately you can conquer it. Then put those notes back into the phrase. Or you can sing a whole section on one vowel instead of the words. This will help you feel what your approach to the problem note should be. Then put the words back.

Once you start singing to a track or with a live instrument, you will tend to sing harder in order to compete with it. Don't push. It's very easy to slide back to your old way of singing to get the volume you want. Keep your focus on singing the way you did in the exercises. You can work on getting the volume after you make sure that you are using the muscles properly.

Stamina

How much you should practice depends partly on how much you are going to be singing. If you are about to do a recording project where you will be singing four or five hours a day you will need to have built your stamina to that point before you start recording. If you are going to be in a musical that rehearses five nights a week and then plays every weekend for six weeks, you don't want to be hoarse by the time the show opens.

In full scale opera productions the leading roles are often double cast because the parts can be too demanding for one person to sing every day. But on their days off, the singers can't stop singing because they wouldn't be in good enough shape for their performance the next day. They exercise, they warm up and then they *think* through their parts. They hear every note in their heads. Every inflection, every pitch, vibrato, sustained notes - they sing it in their minds. Their vocal cords stretch to the pitches but since they aren't putting any air through they aren't wearing themselves out.

You aren't doing opera, but you need to pay attention to how much singing you can do before you start to get tired. You reach a point of diminishing returns: your voice doesn't respond as well, your speaking voice starts to get scratchy, and you are probably doing more harm than good. Stop and rest. If you practice every day, you will be able to sing for longer and longer periods.

Stamina is only one element of what you are working on when you practice. Range, control, tone, pitch, strength are all elements to strive for in practice. As you work through all of your songs and isolate the problem areas, you will train your body to sing correctly. You 'set' the song in your voice - your body automatically sings the way you've trained it to. When you get into rehearsal or performance you won't have to think about your technique but can concentrate on other things.

Adjust For Problems

Sometimes you will get into trouble: you are getting sick, or you shouted yesterday or didn't get enough sleep. Then you have to adjust your practice. Go slower, paying more attention to what you can and cannot do. If the high notes aren't there, don't push for them. Gently stretch the notes you do have. If you have a rehearsal that night, be very aware of your technique even if it means that the performance suffers. Make whatever adjustments you need to make to get through it: change notes that are too high, sing quieter (but not too quietly since that is actually more difficult), skip parts that aren't essential. Think in the long term. You don't want to blow your voice out in rehearsal and then not have it for the show. If you are hoarse you shouldn't sing at all. Take a few days off to give your voice a chance to heal.

In the end, you are the expert on your instrument. If you pay enough attention, you will be able to tell how long to practice, what you need to be working on and when you haven't practiced enough. The stricter you are with yourself about it, the happier you will be onstage or in the studio.

The Artist Formerly Known as "Prince"

Auditions

"Horrific, horrendous, absolutely horrible"

Shirley Manson on her first audition for **Garbage**
from iZine, http://www.thei.aust.com/ireverbhome.html

Photo Credit: Stephane Sednaoui

How do I get control in an audition?

How do I keep my energy going when I'm rejected by another record label?

Auditioning is hard to do. No matter how much you prepare, it rarely seems to go the way you planned. You are nervous. Whatever you don't like about your performance and the way you look, talk, sing or move, seems glaringly obvious. You are being measured against other people whose performances you generally don't see. It's difficult not to feel like a victim of this process in which you seem to have no power and where this decision about your career feels like it's left to someone else.

When you audition for a play or a band, you only have a general idea of what they are looking for. They might want a petite brunette and you are a tall blond so no matter how well you sing, you won't get that part. If they want a tenor and you are a baritone, you shouldn't even be auditioning. They may say that they want a singer like Dolores O'Riordan of the Cranberries but when you get there they are playing so loud you couldn't possibly show them the dynamic variety that your voice is capable of. But in each of these situations you might walk away feeling like *you've failed.* Something is wrong here.

Imagine for a moment that you are watching a young Katherine Hepburn audition for the role of Maria in West Side Story. No matter how good an actress she is, she would probably not get that part. She's not right for it. She's too upper class and feisty where Maria is sweet and innocent. You must understand the kind of personality that you bring to every role you play. Accept it and use it in the audition. Imagine how different Maria would have been if Hepburn had played her.

The same is true for the role you will play in a band. If you have a pretty voice and an easy going personality, you might want to think twice about auditioning for a hard driving rock band. If you want a chance to strut around and wear outrageous clothes, then the acoustic folk duo is not for you.

Confidence

As you become more confident, you become more specific. You are a unique person and you bring your specific personality traits to whatever you do. You bring your history, ideas, emotions and beliefs. Those traits make you interesting. You should use them, rely on them. As an actor you use them to give substance and reality to a character. As a musician you will shape any band you are in with your presence as the frontperson. It's hard to imagine anyone but Gwen Stefani (No Doubt) singing "I'm Just A Girl" because she brought so much of her personality to it.

Once you have this confidence, an audition is an opportunity to apply these traits to a new set of circumstances and see how they fit. How would David Bowie sing a Rolling Stones' song? More contained than Mick Jagger, I'd imagine. That would be interesting. If you can relieve yourself of the pressure of having to fulfill someone else's expectations (the director's, the band members'), especially since you don't know what those expectations are, you can be yourself. If that happens to fit for everyone, then you're right for the job.

David Bowie

Photo Credit: Nina Schultz

That means it has to fit for you too. No matter how much you want to be in a band, I promise you, you don't want to be in the wrong band. When you go for an audition, you should be auditioning them as well. Do you like the songs? Are the people easy to get along with or do they have attitude problems? Do they show up on time, have transportation, have good equipment? (You can't imagine the number of drummers who have just hocked their drum sets but will be able to get them out next week. Or guitarists who have to be picked up for every rehearsal because their car broke down.) Do you enjoy working with them? Do you feel comfortable trying new things and making suggestions?

18 ▶ Auditions

In auditioning for theater the circumstances are different but your attitude shouldn't be. Do you actually want this role or are you willing to take anything? Is this company going to move you forward in your career? Will the director help you achieve a great performance or will you be embarrassed to invite the agents who are waiting to see you? You have choices to make and this can give you perspective.

In any situation, you mustn't feel desperate. This is not the last audition you will have, and if you don't fit for this one you will fit the next one. In real estate training classes, they say you have to have nineteen rejections before you get one sale. This is a remarkable viewpoint - you **have** to get rejected, so just keep checking them off. The more rejections you get, the closer you are to the perfect fit.

Each record label has to find artists that fit their roster. They may have to turn down a great artist because the music isn't right for the company, their tastes or their market. Their promotion department might have very strong connections in rock radio but have none in R&B. Or maybe they have too many female artists and are only looking for males. They are looking for someone who is exactly right for them. The same is true for managers, agents and all the other people who might reject you. When you take a rejection personally, you assume that you aren't good enough when that might not be the case at all.

All you need is one 'yes.' But make sure it's from someone who understands what you do and loves it, who will work till they drop because they believe in you. You don't want to get signed to a mega-agent who doesn't have time to get you work or to a record company who ends up shelving your record.

The next time you go into an audition you should think 'do I want this?' and 'is this a good step in my career?'. You won't get everything you go out for, but you won't feel like a victim of the process.

Photo Credit: Naomi Kaltman

The Rolling Stones

Rehearsing Your Performance

"When I'm interpreting a song all the work is done
before I go into the studio.
I develop - like any actor would do - a subtext.
I take the original song and understand all the things
about that song that moved me in the first place to want to sing it.
The origin, sense, emotion, meaning of it, the perception
and the dimension of the person who sang it.
Then I add my own contribution, superimposing myself
rather than repeating or annihilating the original."

k.d. lang
from iZine, http://www.thei.aust.com/ireverbhome.html

Photo Credit: Albert Sanchez

Rehearsing Your Performance

20

How do I get my band to <u>perform</u> onstage rather than just play?

How do I sing the same song night after night and still feel it?

Photo Credit: Cindy Palmano

Tori Amos

Life on stage is very different from ordinary daily life. When Tori Amos is on stage, she isn't a regular person behaving in a normal way. Her ability to transcend the petty details of her life and show us her vision of what it means to be human is the reason why she stands on stage in the light while the audience pays money to sit in the dark and watch. Everything she does - her facial expressions, her gestures, her clothing and her songs - supports her vision. There are ways she may act in her everyday life that she doesn't choose to bring on stage, and ways she acts onstage that she wouldn't offstage. Performing is not an ordinary activity. If you are going to perform, you need to prepare for it.

It's hard to practice performing since the only time we really do it is in front of an audience. No matter how much you sing to yourself in the mirror in the privacy of your room, it won't come close to the real thing. The best practice is getting out there on stage.

Rehearsal is the next best thing to being there, provided you actually use the time to rehearse your performance. Few singers actually work out the elements of performance beyond singing. Movements, gestures, interaction with other band members, talk between songs, taking the mic off the stand, running out into the audience—these are not ordinary behavior and they aren't easy. They need practice.

Many singers say they are uncomfortable trying these things in front of their band; they feel embarrassed. But it's hard to imagine a singer being able to try something totally new in front of an audience if they couldn't do it in front of their band. And how will you know if dropping onto your knees is going to work if you don't try it first? The first time Kurt Cobain (Nirvana) jumped from the stage onto a speaker five feet away wasn't in front of an audience. He practiced it first. If you are not getting enough work done in rehearsal, you should consider taking a performance workshop which focuses on developing your stage presence. Then bring your new ideas into rehearsal.

The Emotion Comes First

Practicing your act before you perform it must never lead to a stale mechanized presentation. A memorized gesture that has no feeling behind it looks hollow and vapid. Choreography may be especially susceptible to this danger. The singer seems to be on automatic pilot regurgitating movements that once had meaning. Instead, the songs should generate the emotion which, in turn, generates the movement. Whatever led you to throw your arm in the air and your head back the first time you did it, has to be there every time.

Once you have a wide vocabulary of movements and gestures that you are comfortable with, you can take more chances in your live performances. If you can throw yourself on the floor it is not too hard to writhe to the edge of the stage. If you lean on your guitarist during a solo, you won't be

Kurt Cobain (Nirvana)

Rehearsing Your Performance

embarrassed to rest your head on her shoulder. On the other hand, you must select the options that best express your concept and throw out the rest. It's lovely that you can tap dance but you may not want to include it in your jazz act. Or then again, you might. Once you open the door, the possibilities are endless.

Think Tank

A band can be set up like a think tank in which no idea is ridiculed. When the guitar player puts the guitar over her head and plays her solo backwards, don't tell her it's stupid. Work on developing that idea into something exciting. As a band, you need to give every member permission to do whatever they can think of no matter how absurd. Think of Mick Jagger's shows. He is very loose with his body and he is likely to rub against one of his bandmates. They don't look at him like he's crazy; they allow him to be playful, to try anything. Once there is an atmosphere of creative exploration, then you can select the ideas that will work in performance.

In an ideal situation, your band would know that what you do on stage is separate from reality. As the lead singer, you need to know that you can flirt with the guitarist onstage to illustrate a song, and it won't affect your offstage relationship. It's like a play and the band members are the cast. You aren't going to literally act out the story in the song, but you might use each other to show your emotions. Distinctions between emotions onstage and offstage are difficult to keep in mind. These kinds of agreements need to be made ahead of time.

Tell the band what the mood of each song is, what you are trying to accomplish in it. All of the players should support that mood with their behavior. If the song is bleak and depressing, the bass player and drummer shouldn't be laughing and having fun behind you. If it's romantic the guitarist shouldn't be aggressive and defiant on her solo.

Spontaneity

Spontaneity is a crucial part of a vital stage show. Although I've mostly been talking about very broad gestures that a rock band might use, the ability to respond in a moment to whatever stimulus presents itself is essential for every style of artist. One of the most moving performances I've seen was a very simple and genuine concert by James Taylor. He probably doesn't need to practice his storytelling now that he's done it for so many years, but I'm sure there was a time when he had to structure it without making it sound or feel stiff. Yet there was always room in the structure for him to respond to what was happening around him. Songs like "Fire And Rain" which he had already been doing for years, still felt fresh and real. He didn't do a lot of jumping or running around the stage but what movement he did was heartfelt.

Whatever your personal style, whether it's wild or sedate, fun-loving or serious, you need to be genuinely affected by your material and it has to show. As the front person, the responsibility for a charismatic performance is mainly on your shoulders. You have many elements at your disposal: music, words, arrangements, movements, costumes, attitudes, smoke bombs. Construct a well-practiced framework to perform within, one that's guided by your concept, and it will give you the freedom to improvise.

Photo Credit: Dan Borris

James Taylor

Recording

*"Sometimes I felt like I was going crazy.
It took me six months to record the album,
but I felt like it's taken me thirty-one years to make this album.
There were times when I had to walk away from the microphone
because I was in tears from what I had written, trying to sing it.
And I'd have to come back a few days later to tackle it."*

Janet Jackson about making **"Velvet Rope"**
from Wall of Sound http://www.wallofsound.com

Photo Credit: Mario Testino

Recording ◁ 23

How do I get an emotional take when I'm so concerned with getting a perfect vocal?

What kind of mix do I need in my headphones?

Should I sing the hardest song first to get it over with?

When the time comes for you to record vocals you must be prepared in two main areas:
1. The Technical: vocal technique and studio skills.
2. The Emotional: expression through delivery.

Nothing substitutes for good solid vocal technique. Once you are recording you want to feel confident about your vocal skills. Plan a period of time for pre-production during which you record your rehearsals. You can use a small home four track recorder or even a boombox. Notice pitch problems, sections that are too high or too low, shortness of breath, inconsistent tone, lack of dynamics and vocal strain. These are the kind of problems a voice teacher can help you solve if you address them early enough. A lead singer I worked with recently, who was signed to a record deal on the basis of his live performance, didn't realize that he had vocal problems until he was in the studio. The recording process had to stop while we corrected some old habits that were ruining his pitch and tone.

Improving singing skills takes time, like any instrument. Commit yourself to putting in the necessary hours to insure that your voice will be resilient and strong, able to perform through long hours in the studio, and responsive to the creative ideas you will have. If you are worrying about whether you will be able to hit that high note, you will not be able to be spontaneous in your performance.

Work on the problem spots in the vocal until you automatically do them right. For instance, if you are singing a very long phrase, know where a breath will make sense to the phrasing and still give you enough air to get through the line. If you don't work it out before you record, you will have to make the decision about where to breathe every time you get to that phrase. Ideally the technique should be so ingrained in your body that you will be free to concentrate on the emotion.

Studio Tricks

Once you are in the studio, here are some tips that can help you get a good performance:
1. Take one headphone off and rest it behind your ear. This allows you to hear the tracks and your vocal coming through the phones in one ear and what is coming directly out of your mouth with the other. It usually will improve your pitch.
2. Ask the engineer to adjust the volume of the instruments in your headphones until it is exactly what you need. What you are hearing does not effect the final mix. Singers often need to have their own voices very loud in the headphone mix, so don't be shy about asking for more of your voice.
3. If you are having pitch problems, bring up a chordal instrument, like a keyboard part, in the mix. This will help anchor you in the key. Instruments playing a melodic line might distract you so keep them lower. If you are singing flat, try lowering the volume on most of the instruments to keep you from shouting. This can also be a solution to flat tone. When you shout, you lose resonance as well as any subtlety or dynamic range. Lowering the volume of the track can give you the room to vary your sound.
4. If you are being too careful or singing too quietly, turn up the tracks in your mix.
5. If you are not nailing the track rhythmically, bring up the drums or the bass.
6. Learn good mic technique. If you are singing a loud section, lean back from the mic a few inches; for a quiet section, move into the mic. You don't need to move your feet, just your upper body.

You should test several microphones at the beginning of your sessions, to see which one is the best for your voice. Some will bring out warmth, some brightness, some will make you hiss your 'S's' and some will make you sound boomy. Set up several mics and sing a section of a song through each of them. Then listen to the playback and see which you like best.

24 ▶ Recording

Vocal Fatigue

Another common problem for singers in the studio is vocal fatigue. Put the songs in an order that won't wear you out. Try singing the easiest one first to get you rolling and put you in a good mood, then the hardest while you are still fresh and strong enough to sing it. Then the rest.

It is not uncommon for a singer to sing four to five hours in one session, or more, depending on how long your tone lasts. Your brain might be saying 'I can do it better' but if the engineer tells you that you're losing tone, it's time to stop. How many songs you sing in a session is directly related to your budget. Some projects spend weeks on one vocal track and some will spit out three or four in one long day. Don't expect to go in and sing the song once or twice and be done. It takes a while to get the right sound and levels. Then you have to lock into the feeling, produce a good take and then polish it.

Get Ready

To keep your voice in good shape you need to think about what you eat and drink before and during the session. You should eat a moderate meal that is high in complex carbohydrates and free of dairy three or four hours before recording. Eat lightly while in the studio and drink water (not cold) and herbal tea to keep lubricated. No caffeine, no smoke (yours or anyone else's) and no alcohol. Also be sure to bring something warm to wear; studios are always over-cooled.

Warm up (use **The Singer's Warm-Up CD**) before you start singing so you don't waste a take or two getting your voice going. Warming up should remind your body of how to sing properly so you don't have to think about it while you're performing. Don't abuse your speaking voice the night before or spend the day of the recording talking. If you are using your voice badly all day you will end up losing your voice before the session is over. Often the best and most emotional take is the first one so you should be ready for a full-on performance right from the start.

Live vs. Recorded Performance

It is a good deal easier to give a vital, exciting performance on stage than in the studio. No one notices if you slide to a note, or you scream or your pitches aren't perfect. Your live performance contains many other elements besides your singing: how you look and move, what you say, how you throw your head back or use your hands. The audience is part of the performance, caught up in it like you are. Listening to the CD at home, the audience no longer has your physical presence and energy. They can't see you, they listen more carefully and they can only hear what gets captured on that little piece of tape. Because of the quality of the CD's they buy, they expect a perfect performance.

How do you produce a performance in the studio that is passionate and charismatic when you feel like your voice is under a microscope? You can hear every breath, every missed pitch, every mistake and it makes you self-conscious. Somehow you have to find a balance between spontaneity and control.

Recording Techniques

Basically, there are two ways to record a vocal and most vocals are a combination of the two. The first is to sing it until you get a great take on tape and then go back and fix problem spots in a process called 'punching in'. You sing along with the problem line in the recorded vocal and the engineer records only the spot that needs fixing. The other process is called 'comping': you lay down several takes and then piece together the sections of each that were the best. You might comp a vocal and then go back and punch in on the combined track. Whatever works for you is the way to do it.

Ideally you should try to get a take that is full of fire and personality, even if it has some vocal flubs. Don't stop singing if you make a mistake; it can be fixed later. Keep your focus on the emotion of the song all the way through the take. It is much easier to fix technical problems than it is to insert passion into a technically perfect vocal.

Getting the emotional focus is the hard part. Each song should conjure up a picture or a story for you that makes you feel what you are trying to convey. Create that picture for each song before you come into the studio. And then you have to make the audience feel it with you when you sing.

The singer must have a point of view; he or she can't be an objective observer but must care about what is happening in the lyric. If the song is about how your girlfriend left you, you need to be specific about how that makes you feel: angry? hurt? defiant? If Bono (U-2) were to sing it he would bring his fiery, emotional attitude to it. How will **you** sing it? This is what you bring to the material, how your vision differs from the other singers out there. Take some chances. Once you have a version down on tape that's good, try another one that's completely different. Be emotional; be attitudinal; be hysterical! This is your chance to show us how you see the world.

Most of all remember, this is not your last time in the studio. This is one of a long series of recordings in which your goal is to capture where you are right now. Hopefully you will be recording all of your life, taking steps in the lifelong process of making music.

Ready, Set, Perform

*"…I felt completely spent, like I didn't know who I was
or what I was doing anything for anymore.
And it took me a long time just to become whole again, really.
I tried to write songs and it was disastrous;
I wasn't writing from any place of honesty.
I was trying to force it, because I had all this pressure on me,
or so I thought.
It was mostly self-imposed:
'Oh my God, you haven't had a record in so long.
You have to get right back in again.'
And I had nothing to say. I was completely empty.
I had to live again and fill the well up."*

Sarah McLachlan
from Wall of Sound – http://www.wallofsound.com

Ready, Set, Perform

How do I do a good show when I've had a lousy day?

How do I get ready for a show?

A singer has an intense job. No matter what your mood, or how difficult your day, you need to be able to jump up in front of the audience and do a great performance. This means being able to sing the energized uptempo numbers as well as the blues ballads even if your day was right out of a soap opera. You must make a shift from your daily life into a state of mind that transcends the ordinary.

This state of mind is something you need to build. You probably already know what it feels like. It's similar to how you feel when you are writing a song and the next thing you know, hours have gone by. Or, in performance, when you feel so connected to the material that it's effortless. If only we could have that connection whenever we wanted. Every song we write would be stunning, every performance exciting. Without this feeling of connection - to the material, to the moment, to the audience - you can't make the leap to being an 'artist'. During your best performances, you will almost feel that the song travels through you if you just get out of its way. When you realize that your job is to move over and let it work, then you will have a great performance.

Soap Opera Day

But back to the soap opera day. Let's say that your mother called and told you she wouldn't pay for your voice lessons anymore and asked why you don't get a real job. Your significant other is having a temper tantrum because you are gone all the time. Your manager called to say that none of those important people you were counting on can come to the show tonight. What happens to the connection? How can you get into the altered state that gives you the freedom you need on stage, when you are so bogged down in the mire of the soap opera?

You need a process that removes you from your everyday concerns and allows you to remember why you felt connected to those songs in the first place. That connection is what brings you into the present, into being in this moment, with this song and this audience. Being present in this way allows you to be creative and intuitive.

Over many years of performing and in working with my clients, I have developed a process to get from daily life into the mindset needed on stage. It takes getting focused, not being distracted by everyday events or even by the worries of making the performance work. It takes pulling your attention down to the quietest, most centered spot inside you where you know how to find the truth in your performance, where you are sure and confident and, therefore, free. I call this process a 'pre-performance ritual'.

Creating A Ritual

A ritual is something that is done over and over in the same way. It is an ordered sequence of events that helps draw the participant further toward the desired conclusion through repetition. Anything can be a ritual. You come home from work, kiss your mate hello, sit in front of the TV to watch the news and start to relax. Just picturing yourself sitting in your living room can help you start to relax while you're driving home.

Think of a wedding. There are certain things that happen every time. The bride walks down the aisle, usually in white. Certain words are always said, "Do you take this man...?" "I now pronounce you..." The fact that we have heard these words before in this same situation and that we know they are coming give them more power than if we were hearing them for the first time. The symbolism of the events and their familiarity make the meaning of the ceremony more vivid. It connects us emotionally to other weddings that we have experienced.

The process I've created for moving from daily life to performance is a ritual made up of activities that draw me closer to my stage self. Your ritual will probably be different but the idea will be the same. It takes me a little over an hour to do mine but yours can be any length that works. Once I start it, I won't do anything that would draw me out of it, like answer the phone. (That would be like stopping the wedding!)

When you've created a ritual that works for you, you will find that just the act of starting it will bring you closer to a performance state. You know from the beginning that you will end up on stage and each part of it draws you further in. That is how rituals work.

Turn Your Attention To Yourself

Create your own ritual. You might like long hot baths with candles and incense. If you have a lot of nervous energy before a show, jog around the block. The basic premise is to turn your attention to yourself. See how you are feeling; tune up your body and your mind just as you would an instrument.

You will need a quiet, private space. Set aside enough time, turn on the answering machine, close the door to your room. As far as everyone in your house is concerned, you're not home. First do something physical. I love stretching and usually do a 15-minute routine. It's great to engage your body and watch it move, see how it feels today, get out of your mind for a while. Your body, after all, is your instrument and your major means of expression. You should be connected to it. If you like to swim or run, this is the time. If you don't do anything physical, you'd better start. If you are ever in a touring road show or have to tour in support of your record, you will need some kind of exercise to keep your mental health as well as your physical stamina.

After stretching, I do some kind of meditation. If you have just worked up a sweat, you might not want to do this right now, so play with the order of things. Maybe put it after your shower. Some form of meditation is essential; it quiets your mind, relaxes your body and turns you inward. If you have one you like, use it. If not there are books and classes on meditation. It's important to find a meditation you can actually accomplish. It should be simple and easy to do. Remember that the basic idea is to work from the outside world to an inside reality and order your ritual accordingly.

Practice Creativity

I am including a simple meditation here which is in two parts. The first part is the quiet meditation and the second is a creative visualization. Since we don't have many opportunities in daily life to practice creativity, we need to invent some, especially before a performance when spontaneity is so important. Practicing creativity as a part of your pre-performance ritual opens up the creative pathways in the brain so your performances will be more creative.

Sit comfortably in a chair with your feet flat on the ground and your hands in your lap. Close your eyes. Relax your body. You can think about each body part one at a time, relaxing from the toes up. Concentrate on your breathing and try to clear your mind. When you notice your mind wandering bring it back to the breathing again. Think of it as a child you are holding by the hand as you walk through the park. Your objective is to get to the other side of the park but the child keeps running off, fascinated by some new thing. Each time she runs away you gently take her by the hand again and lead her through the park. The child (your mind) is playful and wants to be entertained. Keep bringing your focus back to the breathing. When you feel centered and relaxed, go on to the next part - the creative visualization.

This is where you practice creativity. You can do it anytime, not just before a show. The purpose of it is to spend some relaxed time inside your mind. Imagine whatever you would like to; let your mind wander. Don't feel that you have to force anything to come to you. Your mind has a million images waiting, but you have to relax to get them. Sometimes that means going into the visualization and seeing nothing for a while. But, whatever you see, accept it and let it lead you. There are no right or wrong images; only **your** images.

The Creative Visualization

After you've quieted your mind, remain in the comfortable relaxed position with your eyes closed. Imagine that you are on a lovely path near the ocean. It's a beautiful day. The sun is warm and the sky is blue and you feel very good. As you walk along you see the ocean and the waves gently gliding into the sand. You walk barefooted on the warm sand down toward the water. You can smell the salt in the air and feel the sun on your back. You feel comfortable and at peace. As you walk along the shoreline you see many small shells in the sand and one in particular that is very beautiful. As you walk up to this shell, you grow smaller and smaller, until you are small enough to go inside it. First you walk around the outside and see it's delicate colors and feel the sand where it clings to the shell. You walk around to the front of the shell and stop outside. When you are ready, you will go inside the shell and inside you will find anything you can imagine. It will be completely safe and within your control because everything you find will have been created by you. When you are ready, go inside. Take as long as you like exploring the inside and come back out when you are done.

You step back onto the sand; the sun is warm and there are birds flying overhead. You feel very good. As you walk away from the shell you grow larger and larger until you are back to your normal size. You walk down the shoreline to the path you came on, feeling at peace with yourself. You know you will always be able to come back to your shell whenever you want to.

The first time you do this you might find only the inside of a shell. But as you practice it more and more, you will discover worlds inside your shell. Be patient. And on the days when you don't find anything interesting, don't push your mind for images. Relax and float.

28 ▶ Ready, Set, Perform

All The Rest

After the visualization, lay out your stage clothes. I keep them separate from the clothes I wear everyday. This gives them a certain power when I pull them out of my closet. It means it's almost time. And if your clothes express your stage persona, then when you look at them you should get a good hit of what that persona feels like.

Take a bath or a shower. Use candles, incense - whatever appeals to you. The idea is to treat yourself well, to prepare your body for a special event and to focus on the preparations.

Next, look at your face in a mirror. Really look. Most of the time when we look in a mirror, we pose to try to look good. But that's not what other people see. All of your character, the weaknesses and the strengths, can be seen in your face. I put on make-up and watch my face and talk to myself. Crazy? Maybe. But it works. I start to see how others see me. I watch the transformation from my regular face to my made-up one. It always amazes me. This is also when I vocalize (warm-up my voice). I take lots of time with this step. I'm not done until my voice feels good and my face looks right. Then I get dressed.

After this point, the rest of the world starts to get involved. While driving to the show, listen to a compilation tape that you've made of your currently favorite great performances. As other people start to interfere with your nicely-built calm, you may find that it deteriorates a little. You get to the club or the theater and find you have no dressing room or the booker has changed your performance time. You can't just ignore it all, but if you find yourself unraveling a little you can get reconnected. Fifteen minutes before you go on, go into a cubicle in the bathroom and do a short, but focused, version of your meditation. The feeling of calm will come back and you will be centered again.

Keep At It

You might find the first few times you do this, it doesn't work as well as I'm telling you it will. That's because it takes time and repetition for it to gain strength. You also may find it's hard to **want** to slow down and turn inward. Performing is a very out-going experience. At the theater or the club all your friends will want to say hello and talk to you about things that are unrelated to your gig. You get caught up in the excitement of the moment - although you shouldn't be shouting over the loud music anyway. You may feel that all your adrenaline will be lost if you focus inward. But in reality, the opposite will happen. The adrenaline stays but it's channeled, not scattered. It comes out as powerful, focused personality, as conviction and charisma which is just what you want.

Photo Credit: Kate Garner

"You know,
you can't always expect to be
on the top of the world.
Everybody goes up and down.
That's life.
But the thing is . . .
I love singing.
I love making albums and
we all love [what] we do.
And that, I hope, is obvious."

Dolores O'Riordan (The Cranberries)

from www.celtic-connection.com/music

No Clones

Photo Credit: Anton Corbijn

*"We felt that rock and roll
had gotten too safe
and people knew what the sound
of a Marshall guitar was
when it was turned up to 11.
There was no surprise to it,
so we had to try and start again and
find something fresh which entails,
really, breaking up the band
and starting again
which is what we did for the
'Unforgettable Fire'…"*

Bono (U2)

*from iZine, http://
www.thei.aust.com/ireverbhome.html*

*"Anybody can be clever,
but I think at some point
you have to be pretty committed
to either the character
or the emotion . . .
If you're going to lay
everything out creatively,
it does you well
to know who you are."*

Sheryl Crow

from Grammy Magazine

Photo Credit: Guzman

30 ▶ No Clones

How do I set myself apart from all the other aspiring singers?

How do I get record label interest?

Photo Credit: Naomi Kaltman

Mariah Carey

There is a recurring scenario that I encounter from my vantage point in Los Angeles, where thousands of hopeful singers flock each year. I see talented singers presenting bland or derivative demo tapes. If you sound like the artist you admire or if your songs aren't a specific reflection of your own experience, then you aren't showing the music industry anything they haven't already seen and heard a hundred times before. You need to be an artist first and foremost. Express yourself through your music; show your vision of what it means to be human. Then, even though you are telling **your** story, with the particular details from your experiences, if you say it with conviction and clarity it will resonate for your audience.

Every artist has to find his/her own identity. When novelists develop a recognizable style it is said that they have found their 'voice.' Novelists John Steinbeck and Ernest Hemingway each had a specific style and certain themes that reflected who they were and how they saw life. Painters develop in a similar way. We can distinguish a Van Gogh from a Picasso because their separate visions made their styles and subjects strikingly different.

A singer, a frontperson, a songwriter (even a band) has to evolve this same unique persona. By trying many different musical styles, songs and lyrics to find what works, you can eliminate what doesn't suit you. It won't be enough to find or write a nice song, one you can sing easily and has a good hook. It has to be a great song, a perfect song, one that fits you like a glove. The lyric must say exactly what you want to express, and the melody must be made for your voice. Think of Mariah Carey's first hit "Vision of Love". It showed all of the elements that made her great - intensity, emotion and a spectacular range and technique. Or Sheryl Crow's first hit "Leaving Las Vegas" which reflected her disillusionment and her straightforward, conversational approach.

Most singers try to sound like the records they love, the artists who have influenced them. While imitation feels safe, it is not art, and you must make art. You need to take your own experiences, your own vision, your own voice and create a unique and personal statement.

Your Personality

Ask yourself: "What do I want to say? How am I so special that an audience will buy my records?" Here's an assignment for you: Ask five friends to write down your three strongest personality attributes. Ask them to be very honest and if they are shy about telling you the truth have them seal it in an envelope. These attributes don't need to be positive: if someone thought you were 'pushy', 'aggressive', or 'angry', those might be very useful in a stage persona. On the other hand, 'nice', 'friendly', 'sensitive' are not terribly useful. They aren't big enough to use in lyrics or onstage. Also 'talented', 'original', 'unique' won't help. You wouldn't be onstage in the first place if you didn't have those attributes.

It is difficult to see yourself as others see you but these lists may help. What do people see when they see you onstage or hear your recording? Does it affect them? When you go to a show of an artist that you love, you walk away feeling that they were singing about **your** life, that how they feel is how you feel, and you want to be like them. Does that happen to your audience?

Photo Credit: Neal Preston

Bruce Springsteen

Working Class Hero

Let's look at some artists who have accomplished this. Bruce Springsteen was influenced by other artists and by what was going on around him as he was coming up through the musical ranks in New Jersey. Still, he created his own sound and made his vision of the working class hero popular to a huge audience. His voice was unique and reflected his attitudes – a rough, gritty sound with lots of energy, clearly a man who had to struggle up from the streets. He rarely sang with vibrato or a sweet, round tone because these translate to the listener as relaxed or easy. In Springsteen's voice we heard the tension and conflict in his life.

All of the elements of his music and performance reflected his vision. Working class values were not the normal topic of song lyrics. Sax and organ sounds were considered passé. He re-invigorated roots rock by bringing his very personal, poetic vision to a style of music he loved. He made this vision real to his audience by showing us his experiences through detailed stories from his life. In "My Hometown" his father puts him up behind the wheel of the car to look around at the town. Even though I never had that experience, the image is so strong that the event comes to life for me. This is the job of the artist — to create a personal imagery which is so vivid that it rings for us all.

Photo Credit: Simon Alexander

David Byrne

Pushing The Boundaries

Every major artist has made a strong personal statement whether or not it was a popular point of view at the time. When Madonna first broke into the market with "Borderline" and "Lucky Star" she presented herself as a Boy-Toy, a teasing boy-hungry girl. She dressed in a way that was considered trashy before it was popular: too much jewelry, her navel in every video, suggestive clothing and gestures. Suddenly every adolescent girl in the country dressed like her. She did not represent the prevailing attitude about women. She was pushing the boundaries of what was acceptable as she has done over and over again since.

John Lennon

Most artists present a persona that is in conflict with what society deems acceptable. We don't expect to see an insurance salesman or school teacher on stage at a rock concert unless it's someone like David Byrne making a statement about 'modern man'. Instead we expect a role model who is willing to take a stand, who isn't afraid. What was it about Nirvana that skyrocketed them to fame and fostered so many neo-Nirvanas in their wake? They were aggressive, noisy, belligerent and defiant and they filled a need in millions of listeners. They were not ordinary.

Where You Stand

Each artist pushes the boundaries in different ways: some like Springsteen with social themes, some like The Artist Formally Known as "Prince" with sexual attitudes. Sheryl Crow is a cynical party girl. Suzanne Vega is a street poet. What these artists have in common is their willingness to take big risks, to stand behind and sing about what they love (or hate) and believe in. Elvis Presley, John Lennon, Patsy Cline – they each stand for something in our minds. What do you stand for? Who do you present?

Your own personal statement is found not only in lyrics but in every aspect of your presentation. Is the music driving or sweet? Do you wear spurs or army boots? Are you excitable or calm? Every detail adds up to the total picture your audience will have of you down to the flyers you mail out for the gigs. These elements will evolve as your concept becomes clearer. You must set yourself apart from all the other talented, ambitious singers, and you can do that by being completely yourself. Show us the world as you see it. Present yourself to us with all your idiosyncrasies. Take a stand — musically, lyrically and visually. Then you won't be in competition with any other singer, because no one else can be you.

Photography by Rush Studios

Patsy Cline

The Singer's Warm-Up CD

Why, When & How

Why

Your voice depends on several sets of muscles in your body; in order to work properly it needs to be warmed up and stretched before use. Singing is strenuous, as you know if you have ever rehearsed for three hours with a band. You get tired and even hoarse. If you jump right into a rehearsal or performance without warming up you spend the first half hour or so missing pitches, not having range or tone and wearing yourself out.

Warming up is a way of gently stretching and moving your instrument much like a guitarist moves his fingers on the fretboard before playing or a drummer loosens her wrists by tapping the sticks on a table top.

If you find yourself straining for the high notes in the third hour of rehearsal, or if you wake up in the morning (or afternoon) after a show and it takes a little more effort to talk, or if it takes you a couple of songs for your voice to really sound right, **you need to be warming up.**

When

On days when you are rehearsing or performing, you should warm up both late morning and evening. (I personally find it very hard to sing the first thing in the morning.) The earlier warm-up should consist of a complete and focused run-through of the Warm-Up CD followed by an a capella version (without instruments) of a song that has lots of vocal jumps and complex licks. Try to focus on your technique instead of getting caught up in the emotion.

Your evening warm-up can usually be shorter if you did a good job earlier in the day and have been singing all day. Eventually you will be able to tell how much additional warm-up you need: fifteen or twenty minutes of those exercises that work the best for you should be enough, especially if you do them right before performing. If you feel particularly tight after a performance or rehearsal, do the warm-up again to stretch back out.

On days when you don't have any strenuous singing to do, you should work on the problem areas of your voice. Some of these you can see for yourself: is your pitch accurate? is your range large and flexible? do you have the power you need? Some problems you will need a voice teacher to uncover: is your throat tight? do you breathe incorrectly? are you straining? See the section on how to find a voice teacher.

A good voice teacher will work with you on these problems and give you a tape to work with at home. Before you do their tape, warm-up. After you do your lesson tape, sing. If you are singing to a recording that has a vocal on it, turn it down so you can hear yourself and try to sing the song applying the techniques you've been working on.

Exercising is not too exciting but progress is. You'll watch your voice take shape in just weeks if you are diligent about practicing.

How

Program one of **The Singer's Warm-Up CD** has the exercises and the instructions on how to do them. It takes each pattern up in half steps but does not take them back down. You can stop the CD at the end of each set and work yourself down the scales. Program two has very little instruction and has the patterns going both up and down.

Work with program one until you feel very familiar with the instructions. The exercises only help if you know what to concentrate on. Doing them on 'automatic pilot' does very little. Once you feel that you understand the purpose of each exercise, you can go on to program two and do them without instructions.

Please remember that all voices are different and you may not go as high as the exercises go on the CD. Stop if it gets too high or too low. If an exercise hurts or is tiring, skip it. Feel free to change things to make them work better for you - change the order or drop the consonant. On the other hand if you feel that you can go higher or lower without straining, turn off the CD and try it. You are the expert on your instrument.

You also may find that you can go higher one day than the next. This is normal since your voice is affected by so many things around you, i.e. the weather, your health, your emotional state, what you ate, and many more elements. Don't push yourself today to do what you could do yesterday and will probably be able to do again tomorrow.

Breath Control

Breathing is the single most important element in singing. In order to control your voice you have to put out exactly the amount of breath you need for the sound you want. That breath needs to be as focused as a laser beam. How you exhale controls the quality of the sound, the volume and, in part, controls the pitch and the tone. How you inhale governs how you exhale.

Most people in their everyday lives inhale into their upper lungs i.e., their shoulders go up as does their chest. When the air is in your upper lungs, you don't have the kind of detailed control of it that you need. The muscles available to control the air are the wrong ones: throat, jaw and tongue muscles. These little tiny muscles are easy to find when you want your sound to be louder or higher but they will wear you out and cause serious vocal problems. A singer (or a swimmer or runner —anyone who has to control their air) should fill their lower lungs allowing the bigger, stronger muscles of your abdomen and diaphragm to do the work. This means that instead of a breath that is vertical, with your chest filling with air and expanding upwards, the breath should be horizontal, with your stomach expanding outwards.

Test Yourself

Put one hand on your abdomen and the other hand on your back, both at about waist level. Inhale by filling your lower lungs with air so that your hands move apart. As you exhale let your stomach go back in gently. Think of your stomach as a balloon that inflates and deflates. Your chest shouldn't move, not even an eighth of an inch. As you get better at this, your back will also move out when you inhale. Try putting your thumbs one on each side of your spine, at about waist level. Relax your shoulders. Now inhale into your thumbs. This helps you feel the outward movement of your back.

Lie down on your back. Relax for a minute. After a few seconds you will notice that you are breathing into your abdomen. When we were infants, this was the natural way to breathe, but as we age and our stress levels increase, our breathing tends to move upwards. Unfortunately, you might lose the abdominal breathing once you stand up, but with practice it will become natural again.

Fiery Breath

Here is an exercise called Fiery Breath, to help you get comfortable with this new way of breathing. Put one hand on your abdomen. Inhale into your abdomen and exhale forcibly so that your stomach muscles push in and the air comes out suddenly. Repeat this—inhale, abdomen out, exhale forcibly, abdomen in—thirty times picking up the tempo as you get comfortable with it. Breathe through your mouth. As you go faster you may find that you've fallen back into the old habit of breathing vertically again. In that case, stop and start over by breathing slowly and gently into your lower lungs until you have the feeling again.

Fiery Breath is only meant to make inhaling properly more intuitive. When you sing, **you don't need to exhale forcibly.** There is very little need for a great deal of air pressure if you have a strong voice. It is very easy to get hooked on the feeling of 'pushing' a lot of air into your vocal cords and actually it can be very harmful. Your vocal cords will tend to tense against all the air you are shoving into them instead of stretching to the pitch. Singing requires finesse.

Try singing a song a capella (without instruments). Think about your breathing. Initially you may feel that you can't get enough air, but that is because your lung capacity is underdeveloped. Your lower lungs will stretch out and your ribs in the back will loosen up and make room for the larger inhalation. This way of breathing will become intuitive and you won't have to think about it while you sing. If you breathe properly and don't use the muscles in your throat, tongue and jaw to control the air, you will find that you have a lot more air to use but you don't need as much.

The Diaphragm

The diaphragm is a muscle that sits below your lungs and causes them to fill with air. Once you put the air in the right place, you must learn to control it with your diaphragm and abdominal wall. This is what is meant by the expression 'breathe from your diaphragm'. Not only do these muscles need to be strong enough to give you power and volume, but they need to have even more control and strength when you want to sing a fast and accurate lick, or a big jump in pitch, or very, very quietly. Building strength and control begins with proper breathing.

Be patient with yourself. After breathing vertically thousands of times a day all the years of your life, a new way to breathe takes lots of concentration. Remember that your voice is an instrument like any other. It takes time to learn to play it – time and patience and practice.

The Exercises

Although I do not recommend playing an instrument while warming up your voice – you can't concentrate as well – for those of you who want to follow along on an instrument, here is a written version of the exercises as they appear on the CD. Full instructions are not included here, just brief reminders. The exercises are written here in the key of 'C' although that may not be the key where they actually start on the CD.

Singer's Warm-Up CD For Men Or Women

(ed. note: the order may be slightly different on your CD.)

Program One

1. Work begins with a chest voice exercise using the vowel sound 'ah'.

2. Again in chest this time on the vowel 'oh'.

3. Now we move into head voice using the sound 'oo' like in 'tooth'.

4. Next is the waterfall.

5. I call this one the 'long pattern' and we do it now on 'koo', going back and forth between chest and head.

At the end of this exercise I tell you about several other versions of this pattern that we will do on program two on the CD.

6. We do the waterfall again so you can work on it in reverse.

7. This next exercise loosens up your throat by making you sing in your nose.. On 'mmm'.

8. This is similar to #7 but works a larger section of your voice. On 'mum'.

9. After warming up and working your chest and head voices individually, we now want to work on building a blended sound between them. Sing this exercise on 'ma'.

10. To make your voice flexible and accurate, we will do this light and fast exercise which begins in head but goes to chest on the bottom. The vowel is 'ee'.

11. In chest again, we work your voice down as far as it will go. Gently sing the sound 'ah'.

12. The 'glottal fricative' helps relax your voice after you've been working high or hard. Try it after a rehearsal.

That's it. You're done with your warm up.

Program Two

In the first program, the exercises are in an order that will help you learn them. Now that you know what you are doing, the order in the second program is different in order to best warm you up.

1. The waterfall on 'oo'.

2. The waterfall going up on 'oo'.

3. In head on 'oo'.

4. The long pattern on 'koo'.

On the way down, hold the top for two long counts.

5. In chest on 'ah'.

6. In chest on 'oh'.

7. The long pattern on lips. You can use your fingers to lift the corners of your mouth.

On the way down, hold the top for two long counts.

8. The long pattern on rolling tongue.

On the way down, hold the top for two long counts.

9. 'MMM' is the sound. Very nasal.

10. The long pattern on 'mum'.

11. Flexibility on 'ee'.

12. In chest on 'ma'.

13. Down to your lowest note on 'ah'.

14. Everyone's favorite - the 'glottal fricative.'

Now sing !!

Lis Lewis is a voice teacher and performance coach in Los Angeles, CA. She has been training recording artists for over 30 years. Her web site, **The Singers' Workshop**, is loaded with insider information for pop singers of all styles (www.TheSingersWorkshop.com). Lis is the author of the books *The Singer's First Aid Kit* and *The Pop Singers Warm-Up*. In addition to private coaching, she has worked in collaboration with managers, record labels, producers, bands and song-writers in the recording and rehearsal studio to get the best performances from their artists.

Lis' clients have included:
• The Pussycat Dolls, The All-American Rejects, Britney Spears, Gwen Stefani, Jimmy Eat World, Jack Black,
  The Panic Channel, Andrew Dice Clay, Taproot, eastmountainsouth, Trapt, Michel'le
• The cast of the CBS TV show *Rock Star: Supernova* including the rockers and the house band
• Band members in Linkin Park, the Dave Navarro band, Journey, Kiss, the Robert Cray band, the Don Henley Band,
  The 'E' Street Band and Alanis Morrisette's band
• Cast members of *The Reba Show, Friends, Ghost Whisperer, Star Trek Deep Space Nine* and
  the Broadway star of *Chicago*

As a visiting lecturer or as an artist-in-residence, Lis has taught at colleges, music conferences and music schools including:
• Paul McCartney's Liverpool Institute of the Performing Arts, Liverpool, England
• Taxi Road Rally, Los Angeles, CA
• UC Berkeley Extension, Berkeley, CA
• UCLA Extension, Los Angeles, CA
• Musician's Institute, Los Angeles, CA;
• The Blue Bear School of Music, San Francisco, CA.

Lis can be reached at:
The Singers' Workshop
4804 Laurel Canyon Blvd., #123
North Hollywood, CA 91607
(818) 623-6668
http://www.thesingersworkshop.com
lis@thesingersworkshop.com.

The Angel City Voice

Should you make a CD?
What is mastering?
When do you need an agent?
What should you never eat before you go onstage?

The Angel City Voice is the newspaper for pop singers, with interviews, information, humor and articles on such subjects as touring, vocal health, management, band relations, auditioning and much more.

To subscribe and receive six issues a year, please fill out the form below and send with a check or money order for $10 U.S. *(A subscription in Canada is $12 US/year. In all other parts of the world a subscription is $16 US/year.)* to:

─── Order Form ───

The Angel City Voice

4804 Laurel Canyon Blvd., #123
Valley Village, CA 91607
U.S.A.

Name _____

Address _____

Address _____

City, State, Country, Zip _____

Phone __(____)_____

Comments _____

_____